DK READERS

Pre-level 1

Fishy Tales
Colorful Days
Garden Friends
Party Fun
In the Park
Farm Animals
Petting Zoo
Let's Make Music
Meet the Dinosaurs
Duck Pond Dip
My Dress-up Box
On the Move

Snakes Slither and Hiss
Family Vacation
Ponies and Horses
My Day
Monkeys
John Deere: Busy Tractors
LEGO® DUPLO®: On the Farm
Cuentos de Peces *en español*
Dias Ilenos de color *en español*
Star Wars: Blast Off!
Star Wars The Clone Wars: Don't Wake the
    Zillo Beast!

Level 1

A Day at Greenhill Farm
Truck Trouble
Tale of a Tadpole
Surprise Puppy!
Duckling Days
A Day at Seagull Beach
Whatever the Weather
Busy Buzzy Bee
Big Machines
Wild Baby Animals
A Bed for the Winter
Born to be a Butterfly
Dinosaur's Day
Feeding Time
Diving Dolphin
Rockets and Spaceships
My Cat's Secret
First Day at Gymnastics
A Trip to the Zoo
I Can Swim!
A Trip to the Library
A Trip to the Doctor
A Trip to the Dentist
I Want to be a Ballerina
Animal Hide and Seek
Submarines and Submersibles
Animals at Home
Let's Play Soccer

Homes Around the World
Bugs and Us
LEGO® DUPLO®: Around Town
LEGO® City: Trouble at the Bridge
LEGO® City: Secret at Dolphin Bay
LEGO® Pirates: Blackbeard's Treasure
Star Wars: What is a Wookiee?
Star Wars: Ready, Set, Podrace!
Star Wars: Luke Skywalker's Amazing Story
Star Wars: Tatooine Adventures
Star Wars The Clone Wars: Watch Out for
    Jabba the Hutt!
Star Wars The Clone Wars: Pirates... and
    Worse
Power Rangers: Jungle Fury: We are the
    Power Rangers
Indiana Jones: Indy's Adventures
John Deere: Good Morning, Farm!
A Day in the Life of a Builder
A Day in the Life of a Dancer
A Day in the Life of a Firefighter
A Day in the Life of a Teacher
A Day in the Life of a Musician
A Day in the Life of a Doctor
A Day in the Life of a Police Officer
A Day in the Life of a TV Reporter
Gigantes de Hierro *en español*
Crías del mundo animal *en español*

A Note to Parents

DK READERS is a compelling program for beginning readers, designed in conjunction with leading literacy experts, including Dr. Linda Gambrell, Distinguished Professor of Education at Clemson University. Dr. Gambrell has served as President of the National Reading Conference, the College Reading Association, and the International Reading Association.

Beautiful illustrations and superb full-color photographs combine with engaging, easy-to-read stories to offer a fresh approach to each subject in the series. Each DK READER is guaranteed to capture a child's interest while developing his or her reading skills, general knowledge, and love of reading.

The five levels of DK READERS are aimed at different reading abilities, enabling you to choose the books that are exactly right for your child:

Pre-level 1: Learning to read
Level 1: Beginning to read
Level 2: Beginning to read alone
Level 3: Reading alone
Level 4: Proficient readers

The "normal" age at which a child begins to read can be anywhere from three to eight years old. Adult participation through the lower levels is very helpful for providing encouragement, discussing storylines, and sounding out unfamiliar words.

No matter which level you select, you can be sure that you are helping your child learn to read, then read to learn!

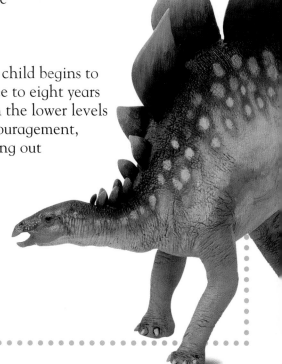

LONDON, NEW YORK, MUNICH,
MELBOURNE, and DELHI

Series Editor Penny Smith
Art Editor Leah Germann
U.S. Editors Elizabeth Hester, John Searcy
DTP Designer Almudena Díaz
Production Angela Graef
Picture Research Myriam Megharbi
Dinosaur Consultant Dougal Dixon

Reading Consultant
Linda Gambrell, Ph.D.

First American Edition, 2006
This edition, 2012
12 13 14 15 16 10 9 8 7 6 5 4 3 2 1
Published in the United States by DK Publishing, Inc.
375 Hudson Street, New York, New York 10014

DK books are available at special discounts for bulk purchases for sale
promotions, premiums, fundraising, or educational use. For details, contact:
DK Publishing Special Markets
375 Hudson Street, New York, NY 10014
SpecialSales@dk.com

A catalog record for this book is available
from the Library of Congress

ISBN: 978-0-7566-9293-3 (pb)
ISBN: 978-0-7566-9292-6 (plc)

Color reproduction by Colourscan, Singapore
Printed and bound in China by L Rex Printing Co., Ltd.

The publisher would like to thank the following for their kind permission
to reproduce their photographs:
a=above; c=center; b=below; l=left; r=right; t=top; b/g=background

Alamy Images: Robert Harding Picture Library Ltd 20-21 b/g, 31cr b/g. **Corbis:**
Matt Brown 26-27 b/g; Larry Lee Photography 18-19 b/g, 30cl b/g; W. Wayne
Lockwood, MD 4-5c b/g, 8-9 b/g; Charles Mauzy 5tcl b/g, 24-25 b/g; Craig
Tuttle 4br b/g, 14-15 b/g, 16-17 b/g, 28-29 b/g, 31bcl b/g; Jim Zuckerman 6-7,
30cb b/g. **DK Images:** Jon Hughes 4-5c, 8-9. **Getty Images:** J.P. Nacivet 22-23
b/g, 31tr b/g; James Randklev 4c b/g, 10-11 b/g.

All other images © Dorling Kindersley
For more information see: www.dkimages.com

Discover more at
www.dk.com

DK READERS

LEARNING
pre-level
1
TO READ

Meet the
Dinosaurs

DK Publishing

Watch out!
Here come
the dinosaurs.

Here is the scary
Tyrannosaurus
[tie-RAN-uh-SORE-us].
It has sharp teeth.

Tyrannosaurus

teeth

Here is the huge
Brachiosaurus
[BRAK-ee-oh-SORE-us].
It has a long neck.

Brachiosaurus

neck

Here is the tough
Triceratops
[try-SAIR-uh-tops].
It has three horns.

Triceratops

horn

Here is the fierce
Velociraptor
[vuh-LOSS-uh-rap-ter].
It has sharp claws.

Velociraptor

claw

crest

Corythosaurus

Here is the noisy
Corythosaurus
[ko-RITH-oh-SORE-us].
It has a bright crest.

Here is the small Compsognathus [KOMP-sug-NAY-thus]. It runs fast.

foot

Compsognathus

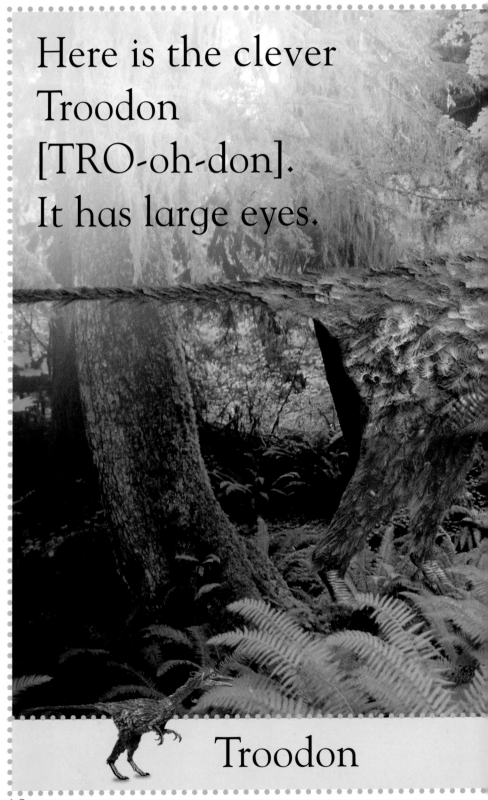

Here is the clever
Troodon
[TRO-oh-don].
It has large eyes.

Troodon

eye

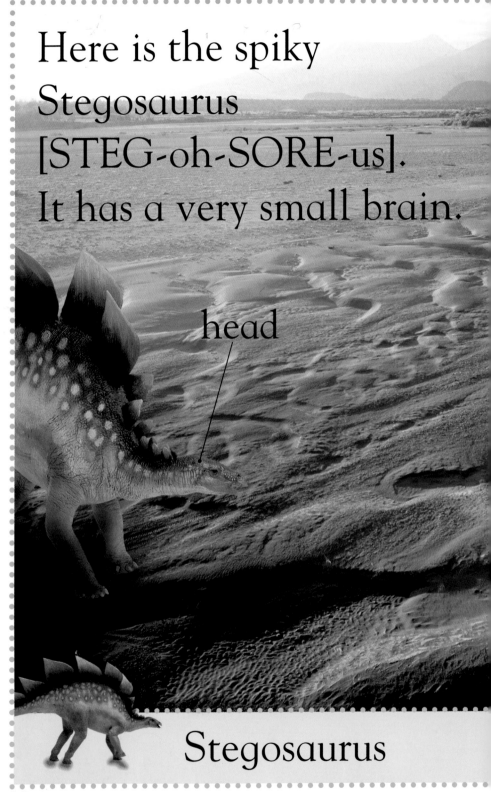

Here is the spiky Stegosaurus [STEG-oh-SORE-us]. It has a very small brain.

head

Stegosaurus

Here is the bird-like Gallimimus [GAL-uh-MIME-us]. It has thin legs and a beak.

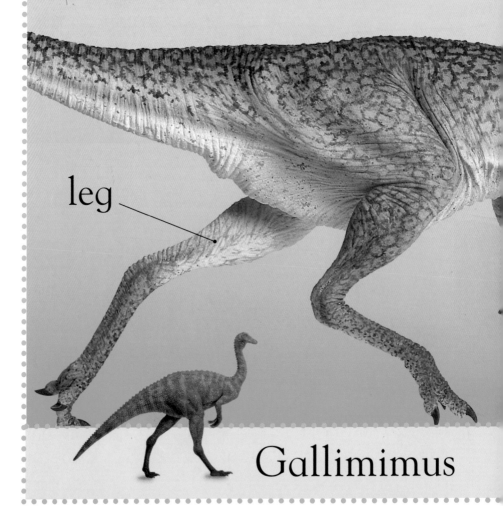

leg

Gallimimus

beak

spike

Iguanodon

Here is the strong
iguanodon
[ig-WAHN-oh-don].
It has a spike on
each thumb.

Here is the plant-eater,
Stegoceras
[ste-GOSS-er-us].
It has a thick skull.

skull

Stegoceras

Here is the armored
Ankylosaurus
[an-KIE-loh-SORE-us].
It has a tail club.

Ankylosaurus

club

Which dinosaur
do you like best?
The one who is...

clever?

scary?

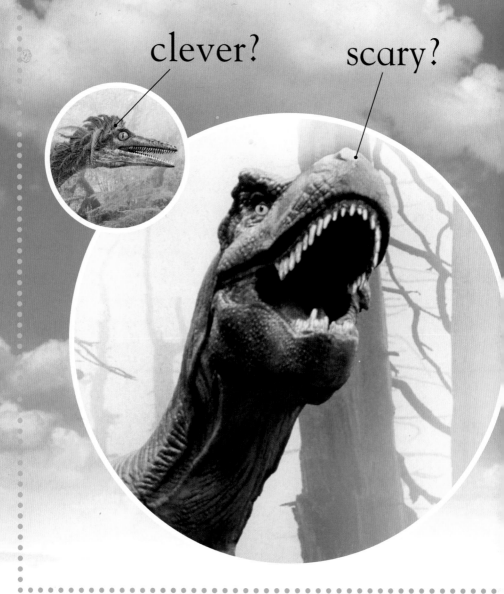

bird-like?

spiky?

noisy?

31

Glossary

Ankylosaurus
a plant-eating dinosaur with a tail-club

Brachiosaurus
a very tall plant-eating dinosaur

Triceratops
a plant-eating dinosaur with three horns

Tyrannosaurus
a large meat-eating dinosaur

Velociraptor
a fast and agile meat-eating dinosaur

Index